UNIT 2

A Million to One

INTER·Active

Mathematics

Activities & Investigations

GLENCOE
McGraw-Hill

New York, New York   Columbus, Ohio   Woodland Hills, California   Peoria, Illinois

Send all inquiries to:
Glencoe/McGraw-Hill
936 Eastwind Drive
Westerville, OH 43081

ISBN: 0-02-824722-1 (Student Resource Book)
ISBN: 0-02-824175-4 (Teacher's Edition)

7 8 9 10   071/043   01 00 99 98

CONTENTS

UNIT 2

A MILLION TO ONE
NUMBER SENSE

Interdisciplinary Applications

DAVID FOSTER

"The national goal is to develop mathematical power for all students. My vision for learning mathematics includes a student-oriented classroom culture, where students are taking charge of their own learning and are actively engaged in a curriculum that reflects today's world, not the mathematics of 150 years ago."

David Foster

**Former Teaching Consultant
Middle Grades Mathematics
Renaissance
Morgan Hill, California**
Author of Units 1, 2, 5, 6, 7, 8, 10, 11, 13, 15, 16, 17, and 18

David Foster received his B.A. in mathematics from San Diego State University and has taken graduate courses in computer science at San Jose State University. He has taught mathematics and computer science for nineteen years at the middle school, high school, and college level. Mr. Foster is a founding member of the California Mathematics Project Advisory Committee and was Co-Director of the Santa Clara Valley Mathematics Project. Most recently, he has taken the position of Consulting Author for Glencoe Publishing. Mr. Foster is a member of many professional organizations including the National Council of Teachers of Mathematics and regularly conducts in-service workshops for teachers. He is also the author of a book on computer science.

SANDIE GILLIAM

"Many students only see mathematics as isolated number facts and formulas to memorize. By using this program, which incorporates the mathematics into a context of large, real-life units tied together with literature, science, and history, the middle school student can find meaning in the mathematics."

Sandie gilliam

**Mathematics Teacher
San Lorenzo Valley High School
Felton, California**
Co-author of Unit 14

Sandie Gilliam received her B.A. from San Jose State University and is a mentor teacher and instructor for the Monterey Bay Area Mathematics Project. She was a semi-finalist for the Presidential Award for Excellence in the Teaching of Mathematics in the state of California. Ms. Gilliam has served as a consultant for the California Department of Education and many local school districts and county offices of education. She is a member of the National Council of Teachers of Mathematics and is a frequent speaker at conferences and teacher in-service workshops. Ms. Gilliam was a writer and consultant for Glencoe's *Investigating Mathematics: An Interactive Approach.*

JACK PRICE

"This program is designed to help students become mathematically powerful as they develop problem-solving skills and self-reliance, as well as the ability to work well with others. At the same time, they will strengthen their basic skills and be exposed to new and exciting ideas in mathematics."

Jack Price

**Co-Director, Center for Science
and Mathematics Education
California State Polytechnic
University
Pomona, California**
Author of Unit 3

Jack Price received his B.A. from Eastern Michigan University and his Doctorate in Mathematics Education from Wayne State University. Dr. Price has been active in mathematics education for over 40 years, 38 of those years at grades K through 12. In his current position, he teaches mathematics and methods courses for preservice teachers and consults with school districts on curriculum change. He is president of the National Council of Teachers of Mathematics, is a frequent speaker at professional conferences, conducts many teacher in-service workshops, and is an author of numerous mathematics instructional materials.

INTERACTIVE MATHEMATICS AUTHORS

KAY McCLAIN

"Building conceptual understanding in mathematics challenges us to re-define what it means to know and do mathematics. This program was developed to allow teachers to become facilitators of learning while students explore and investigate mathematics — strengthening their understanding and stimulating interest."

Kay McClain

Doctoral Candidate
George Peabody College
Vanderbilt University
Nashville, Tennessee
Author of Unit 9, Co-author of Unit 14

BARNEY MARTINEZ

"Students learn mathematics best when their teacher enables them to become actively involved in worthwhile mathematical investigations. Students should be encouraged to interact with each other. Then, through their collaborative efforts, students build their own understanding of mathematics."

Barney Martinez

Mathematics Teacher
Jefferson High School
Daly City, California
Co-Author of Unit 12

LINDA DRITSAS

"This program is designed to encourage students to be creative and inventive, while gaining mathematical power. Open-ended situations and investigations provide the setting that allows students to work at varying depths, while nurturing their natural curiosity to learn."

Linda Dritsas

Mathematics Coordinator
Fresno Unified School District
Fresno, California
Author of Unit 4, Co-author of Unit 12

Kay McClain received her B.A. from Auburn University and her Educational Specialist degree from the University of Montevallo in Montevallo, Alabama. While a teacher at Mountain Brook Middle School in Birmingham, she received the Presidential Award for Excellence in the Teaching of Mathematics in the state of Alabama. Ms. McClain is a Woodrow Wilson fellow and a member of the National Council of Teachers of Mathematics. She regularly conducts teacher in-service workshops and is a frequent speaker at local, state, and national mathematics education conferences. She is also an author of middle school mathematics instructional materials.

Barney Martinez received his B.S. in mathematics from The University of San Francisco and is an instructor of pre-service mathematics teachers at the College of Notre Dame in Belmont, California. Mr. Martinez currently serves on the Mathematics Development Team of the California Department of Education and the Pursuing Excellence Revision Advisory Committee. He is a member of the National Council of Teachers of Mathematics and is very active as a speaker and workshop leader at professional development conferences.

Linda Dritsas received her B.A. and M.A. from California State University at Fresno. She taught middle school mathematics for many years and, for two years, taught mathematics at California State University at Fresno. Ms. Dritsas has been the Central Section President of the California Mathematics Council and is a member of the National Council of Teachers of Mathematics and the Association for Supervision and Curriculum Development. She frequently conducts mathematics teacher in-service workshops and is an author of numerous mathematics instructional materials, including those for middle school students and teachers.

Each of the Consultants read all 18 units while each Reviewer read one unit. The Consultants and Reviewers gave suggestions for improving the Student Resource Books, Teacher's Editions, Cooperative Group Cards, Posters, and Transparencies. The Writers wrote the Student Diversity Strategies that appear in the Teacher's Edition.

CONSULTANTS

Dr. Judith Jacobs, *Units 1-18*
Director, Center for Science
and Mathematics Education
California State
Polytechnic University
Pomona, California

Dr. Cleo M. Meek, *Units 1-18*
Mathematics Consultant,
Retired
North Carolina Dept. of
Public Instruction
Raleigh, North Carolina

Beatrice Moore-Harris,
Units 1-18
College Board Equity 2000
Site Coordinator
Fort Worth Independent
School District
Fort Worth, Texas

Deborah J. Murphy, *Units 1-18*
Mathematics Teacher
Killingsworth Jr. High School,
ABC Unified School District
Cerritos, California

Javier Solorzano, *Units 1-18*
Mathematics Teacher
South El Monte High School
South El Monte, California

WRITERS

Student Diversity
Teacher's Edition

Dr. Gilbert J. Cuevas
Professor of Mathematics
Education
University of Miami
Coral Gables, Florida

Sally C. Mayberry, *Ed.D.*
Assistant Professor
Mathematics/Science
Education
St. Thomas University
Miami, Florida

REVIEWERS

John W. Anson, *Unit 11*
Mathematics Teacher
Arroyo Seco Junior High
School
Valencia, California

Laura Beckwith, *Unit 13*
Mathematics Department
Chairperson
William James Middle School
Fort Worth, Texas

Betsy C. Blume, *Unit 6*
Vice Principal/
Director of Curriculum
Valleyview Middle School
Denville, New Jersey

James F. Bohan, *Unit 11*
Mathematics K-12 Program
Coordinator
Manheim Township School
District
Lancaster, Pennsylvania

Dr. Carol Fry Bohlin, *Unit 14*
Director, San Joaquin Valley
Mathematics Project
Associate Professor,
Mathematics Education
California State University,
Fresno
Fresno, California

David S. Bradley, *Unit 9*
Mathematics
Teacher/Department
Chairperson
Jefferson Jr. High
Kearns, Utah

Dr. Diane Briars, *Unit 9*
Mathematics Specialist
Pittsburgh City Schools
Pittsburgh, Pennsylvania

INTERACTIVE MATHEMATICS CONTRIBUTORS

Jackie Britton, *Unit 18*
Mathematics Teacher
V. W. Miller Intermediate
Pasadena, Texas

Sybil Y. Brown, *Unit 8*
Mathematics Teacher
Franklin Alternative Middle
School
Columbus, Ohio

Blanche Smith Brownley, *Unit 18*
Supervising Director of
Mathematics (Acting)
District of Columbia Public
Schools
Washington, D.C.

Bruce A. Camblin, *Unit 7*
Mathematics Teacher
Weld School District 6
Greeley, Colorado

Cleo Campbell, *Unit 15*
Coordinator of Mathematics,
K-12
Anne Arundel County
Public Schools
Annapolis, Maryland

Savas Carabases, *Unit 13*
Mathematics Supervisor
Camden City School District
Camden City, New Jersey

W. Karla Castello, *Unit 6*
Mathematics Teacher
Yerba Buena High School
San Jose, California

Diane M. Chase, *Unit 16*
Mathematics Teacher/
Department Chairperson
Pacific Jr. High School
Vancouver, Washington

Dr. Phyllis Zweig Chinn, *Unit 9*
Professor of Mathematics
Humboldt State University
Arcata, California

Nancy W. Crowther, *Unit 17*
Mathematics Teacher
Sandy Springs Middle School
Atlanta, Georgia

Regina F. Cullen, *Unit 13*
Supervisor of Mathematics
West Essex Regional Schools
North Caldwell, New Jersey

Sara J. Danielson, *Unit 17*
Mathematics Teacher
Albany Middle School
Albany, California

Lorna Denman, *Unit 10*
Mathematics Teacher
Sunny Brae Middle School
Arcata, California

Richard F. Dube, *Unit 4*
Mathematics Supervisor
Taunton High School
Taunton, Massachusetts

Mary J. Dubsky, *Unit 1*
Mathematics Curriculum
Specialist
Baltimore City Public Schools
Baltimore, Maryland

Dr. Leo Edwards, *Unit 5*
Director, Mathematics/
Science Education Center
Fayetteville State University
Fayetteville, North Carolina

Connie Fairbanks, *Unit 7*
Mathematics Teacher
South Whittier Intermediate
School
Whittier, California

Ana Marina C. Gomezgil, *Unit 15*
District Translator/Interpreter
Sweetwater Union
High School District
Chula Vista, California

Sandy R. Guerra, *Unit 9*
Mathematics Teacher
Harry H. Rogers Middle
School
San Antonio, Texas

Rick Hall, *Unit 4*
Curriculum Coordinator
San Bernardino County
Superintendent of Schools
San Bernardino, California

Carolyn Hansen, *Unit 14*
Instructional Specialist
Williamsville Central Schools
Williamsville, New York

Jenny Hembree, *Unit 8*
Mathematics Teacher
Shelby Co. East Middle
School
Shelbyville, Kentucky

Susan Hertz, *Unit 16*
Mathematics Teacher
Paul Revere Middle School
Houston, Texas

Janet L. Hollister, *Unit 5*
Mathematics Teacher
LaCumbre Middle School
Santa Barbara, California

Dorothy Nachtigall Hren, *Unit 12*
Mathematics Teacher/
Department Chairperson
Northside Middle School
Norfolk, Virginia

Grace Hutchings, *Unit 3*
Mathematics Teacher
Parkman Middle School
Woodland Hills, California

Lyle D. Jensen, *Unit 18*
Mathematics Teacher
Albright Middle School
Villa Park, Illinois

Robert R. Jones, *Unit 7*
Chief Consultant,
Mathematics, Retired
North Carolina Department
of Public Instruction
Raleigh, North Carolina

Mary Kay Karl, *Unit 3*
Mathematics Coordinator
Community Consolidated
School District 54
Schaumburg, Illinois

Janet King, *Unit 14*
Mathematics Teacher
North Gulfport Junior High
Gulfport, Mississippi

Franca Koeller, *Unit 17*
Mathematics Mentor Teacher
Arroyo Seco Junior High
School
Valencia, California

Louis La Mastro, *Unit 2*
Mathematics/Computer
Science Teacher
North Bergen High School
North Bergen, New Jersey

Patrick Lamberti, *Unit 6*
Supervisor of Mathematics
Toms River Schools
Toms River, New Jersey

Dr. Betty Larkin, *Unit 14*
Mathematics Coordinator
K - 12
Lee County School District
Fort Myers, Florida

Ann Lawrence, *Unit 1*
Mathematics
Teacher/Department
Coordinator
Mountain Brook Jr. High
School
Mountain Brook, Alabama

Catherine Louise Marascalco,
Unit 3
Mathematics Teacher
Southaven Elementary
School
Southaven, Mississippi

Dr. Hannah Masterson, *Unit 10*
Mathematics Specialist
Suffolk Board of
Cooperative Education
Dix Hills, New York

Betty Monroe Nelson, *Unit 8*
Mathematics Teacher
Blackburn Middle School
Jackson, Mississippi

Dale R. Oliver, *Unit 2*
Assistant Professor of
Mathematics
Humboldt State University
Arcata, California

Carol A. Pudlin, *Unit 4*
Mathematics Teacher/
Consultant
Griffiths Middle School
Downey, California

Diane Duggento Sawyer,
Unit 15
Mathematics Chairperson
Exeter Area Junior High
Exeter, New Hampshire

Donald W. Scheuer, Jr., *Unit 12*
Mathematics Department
Chairperson
Abington Junior High
Abington, Pennsylvania

Linda S. Shippey, *Unit 8*
Mathematics Teacher
Bondy Intermediate School
Pasadena, Texas

Barbara Smith, *Unit 1*
Mathematics Supervisor,
K-12
Unionville-Chadds Ford
School District
Kennett Square, Pennsylvania

Stephanie Z. Smith, *Unit 14*
Project Assistant
University of Wisconsin-
Madison
Madison, Wisconsin

Dora M. Swart, *Unit 11*
Mathematics Teacher
W. F. West High School
Chehalis, Washington

Ciro J. Tacinelli, Sr., *Unit 8*
Curriculum Director:
Mathematics
Hamden Public Schools
Hamden, Connecticut

Kathy L. Terwelp, *Unit 12*
K-8 Mathematics Supervisor
Summit Public Schools
Summit, New Jersey

Marty Terzieff, *Unit 18*
Secondary Math Curriculum
Chairperson
Mead Junior High School
Mead, Washington

Linda L. Walker, *Unit 18*
Mathematics Teacher
Cobb Middle School
Tallahassee, Florida

A MILLION TO ONE

Looking Ahead

In this unit, you will see how mathematics can be used to answer questions about large and small numbers. You will experience:

▶ exploring large and small numbers

▶ using logical reasoning, rates, and proportions to make predictions

▶ developing your number sense through explorations involving relative size of numbers

Did You Ever Wonder?

What do mathematics and recycling paper have to do with each other? Turn the page and see how David M. Gochenour of Agoura Hills, California combined the two!

Teens in the News

Featuring: David M. Gochenour
Age: 21
Hometown: Agoura, California
Career Goal: Communications
Interests: Athletics, environmental issues

David Gochenour worked as a student assistant for a math teacher his sophomore and junior years of high school. One day, by accident, David made 300 copies of a paper instead of the 30 he had been asked to make. He was dismayed to think that 270 pieces of paper would be thrown away!

This event led David to begin a recycling program at his school. A local recycling company helped him in his efforts.

With the help of another recycling company, David started a community recycling program. David used the money collected from the recycling companies to start an Environmental Club at his school. This club still runs recycling programs at Westminster High School.

David's interest in the environment continued beyond high school. In the summer of 1992, he attended a YES! camp (Youth for Environmental Sanity). As a member of YES!, David traveled to Australia and New Zealand. He helped young people there begin their own YES! programs.

David is using the math he learned in middle school in his environmental projects. He weighs the materials and calculates how much money will be collected. David is now involved in a worldwide concert series that will donate a percentage of the money raised to YES! So as David continues his recycling projects, he's recycling his math skills too!

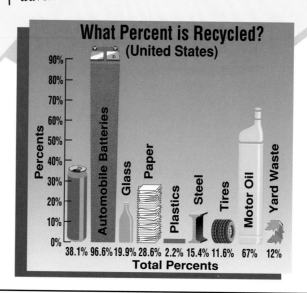

What Percent is Recycled?
(United States)

Automobile Batteries	Glass	Paper	Plastics	Steel	Tires	Motor Oil	Yard Waste
38.1%	96.6%	19.9%	28.6%	2.2%	15.4%	11.6%	67%	12%

Total Percents

Team Project

All That Waste

Suppose every student at your school throws away five sheets of paper a day. In one school year (180 days), how much paper would be thrown away? How much would the paper weigh? How large a landfill would be needed just to hold the paper? How many trees would be needed to make the paper? If the paper were recycled, how much money would your school collect? What could your school do with the money?

Think of other items that could be recycled at school. What local companies could help you in your efforts?

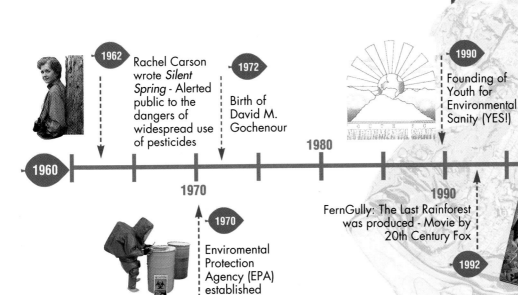

1962 Rachel Carson wrote *Silent Spring* - Alerted public to the dangers of widespread use of pesticides

1972 Birth of David M. Gochenour

1990 Founding of Youth for Environmental Sanity (YES!)

1960

1970

1980

1990

2000

1970 Enviromental Protection Agency (EPA) established

1990 FernGully: The Last Rainforest was produced - Movie by 20th Century Fox

1992

For more information

If you would like more information about starting your own recycling organization, contact:

YOUTH FOR ENVIRONMENTAL SANITY
706 Frederick Street
Santa Cruz, California 95062

You can learn more about the math David used in his recycling program by completing the following activities in this unit.

Setting the Scene

MATHEMATICS TOOLKIT

Erlinda: Hey, what's up?

Many professions require the use of tools. This Mathematics Toolkit includes tools you may find useful as you study this unit. At times you may feel lost or not know where to begin when presented with a problem situation. You should take time to review this and remember the different tools and problem-solving strategies used by the characters in the following script. You don't need to wait until your teacher gives you a hint. Instead, if any approach seems like it will work, try it!

Narrator: Gloria, Mario, and Erlinda are friends. Mario and Gloria are working in the school library on a report about their science experiment.

Mario: That was a cool experiment we did in science with the fruit flies.

Gloria: Yeah, all those flies. It's amazing how quickly they multiplied.

Narrator: Erlinda is not in the same science class as Mario and Gloria. She enters the library and sees her friends.

Mario: Nothing. We're just talking about flies.

Erlinda: Sounds gross.

Gloria: It's not too bad. You keep them in a jar and watch them multiply.

Erlinda: That sounds bizarre!

Mario: Actually, it is pretty cool. We did this experiment in science, where we started with two fruit flies in a jar, and after a month or so, we got a million.

Erlinda: A million?

Gloria: Well, not exactly a million. Mario exaggerates. But a lot.

Mario: You know! There were a lot. In fact, that's what we're doing now.

Erlinda: What's that?

Mario: Well, our class thinks the population of fruit flies must double with each generation to get that many.

Gloria: Yeah, so we need to find out how big the population would be if it doubles every generation.

Erlinda: That doesn't sound too hard.

Mario: Well, our teacher asked us to find the population after one hundred generations.

Gloria: She says that we might see a relationship between that fact and the effects of overpopulation.

Erlinda: Maybe I can help. I hope you have a calculator.

Mario: Yeah, I have one but I'm not sure how to get started with it.

Stop the Script!
Determine the fruit fly population if it starts with two and doubles for 100 generations.

Gloria: We know that we start with two flies and if we double it we have four flies. So after one generation we have four flies.

Family Reunion

Mario: So we just keep doubling it over and over. Like 2, 4, 6, 8,...

Erlinda: No, that's not doubling. That's counting by twos.

Gloria: Oh, doubling is making twice as much. Like 2, 4, 8, 16, 32,...

Erlinda: Right. That's it!

Mario: I see, we just multiply that last answer by 2. I can do that on the calculator.

2 ⨯ 2 ⊟ 4 ⨯ 2 ⊟ 8 ⨯ 2 ⊟ 16 ⨯ 2

Erlinda: Wait, I'll show you an easier way so that you don't have to press the times sign and 2 each time.

Mario: Okay, I'm ready for an easier way.

Erlinda: Most calculators have a constant function. On this calculator you enter the starting number, then the times sign, and then the constant you always want to multiply by. I'll show you. In this case, it doesn't matter because the starting number is 2, and the constant is doubling, which means times two. So enter 2 times 2.

Mario: Yeah, well that's what I did.

Erlinda: I know, but here comes the short cut. All you have to do is just keep pressing the equals sign over and over. Each time you press the equals sign, you get an answer for the next generation.

Mario: Wow! It's working!

Keys pressed	Display
2 ⨯ 2 ⊟	4
⊟	8
⊟	16
⊟	32
⊟	64
⊟	128
⊟	256
⊟	512
⊟	1024
•	•
•	•
•	•

Gloria: Great, now all we have to do is count the times you press the equals sign up to 100. Does this work on all calculators?

Erlinda: Almost all calculators have a constant function. Some you enter the constant value first, others you enter the constant value as the second number. Other calculators have a K key and you enter the constant value either before or after pressing that key. It depends on the calculator.

Mario: Oh no.

Gloria: What happened?

Mario: The calculator broke. The number must have gotten too big! Look, do you see that weird number? It turned into a decimal!

Narrator: The calculator shows the following numbers.

$$1.71798692 \quad 10$$

Erlinda: It's okay, that's just E notation.

Mario: What's that?

Gloria: I know. When the numbers in the calculator get too big or too small for the display, the calculator switches to E notation so we can still do calculations. E notation is a kind of abbreviation for large and small numbers.

Erlinda: Yeah, E notation is the same thing as writing a number in scientific notation. Remember when we learned about scientific notation in science class? You would write this number as $1.71798692 \times 10^{10}$. The number 10 on the calculator becomes the exponent in scientific notation.

Mario: So how does it work?

Gloria: Well, the number in decimal form needs to be switched to a normal number by moving the decimal point over to the right the number of places written at the right. So for your number: $1.71798692 \quad 10$ is really 17,179,869,200

I just moved the decimal to the right ten places. You can see I had to add two zeros to hold the two places at the end of the number. The number is rounded, but we can still get a good approximation.

Erlinda: Yeah, that number is more than 17 billion.

Mario: I know! Seventeen billion fruit flies and I am only on the thirty-third generation.

Gloria: Keep going. Let's get the answer.

Mario: Okay, here it is.

Narrator: Mario's calculator shows the following number.

2.5353012   30

Mario: So, I need to move the decimal point 30 places to the right. There are seven places already behind the decimal, so I need to add 23 more zeroes. Wow! Look at this number. After 100 generations, we would have 2,535,301,200,000,000,000, 000,000,000,000 flies!

Erlinda: Gee whiz, that number is huge and that many flies, oh gross!

Mario: Talk about population explosion! If that were true about fruit flies, we wouldn't be able to live on this planet.

Gloria: No wonder we have to be concerned about overpopulation.

Erlinda: Really. Everyone should understand the danger involved. The numbers can get so big so fast.

Mario: Wow, that was pretty cool using the calculator. I didn't know it could do so much.

This concludes the Mathematics Toolkit. It included many mathematical tools for you to use throughout this unit. As you work through this unit, you should use these tools to help you solve problems. You may want to explain how to use these mathematical tools in your journal. Or you may want to create a toolkit notebook to add mathematical tools you discover throughout this unit.

More Milk Please

Y ou've probably never thought twice about the lid on a gallon of milk. In this activity, you're going to do some big thinking about milk lids.

Together with your group, discuss each question below and arrive at an estimate for each one. Make sure you base your estimates on mathematics.

- How long do you think it would take your math class to collect exactly one million milk lids?

- What container would you use to store all of them?

- Suppose your class actually collected one million milk lids. How long would it take you to count them?

Now think bigger....

- How long would it take your math class to collect exactly one billion milk lids?

- What container would you use to store all of them?

- Suppose your class actually collected one billion milk lids. How long would it take you to count them?

Now think even bigger....

- How long would it take your math class to collect exactly one trillion milk lids?

- What container would you use to store all of them?

- Suppose your class actually collected one trillion milk lids. How long would it take you to count them?

Be prepared to present your findings to the class. You will need to explain how you arrived at each of your estimates.

MENU
station

A

Mr. Big Stuff
Cover Up

1 **U**sing poster board, trace the hand of one person in your group.

2 **E**stimate how many handprints it would take to cover the walls of your classroom.

My Cup Runneth Over

On the table, you will see one jar with beans, one jar with rice and one jar with popcorn kernels. Without counting, use any of the measuring cups provided to come up with an estimate for each question below.

1 **H**ow many beans are in the jar?

2 **H**ow many pieces of rice are in the jar?

3 **H**ow many kernels of popcorn are in the jar?

4 **E**xplain how you arrived at your estimates.

MENU station

Going to Great Lengths

1 **S**uppose you measure one million inches from the front of the school to some location. Where would you end up at the end of those one million inches? Name the location.

2 **S**uppose you measure off one billion inches from the front of the school to some location. Where would you end up at the end of those one billion inches? Name the location.

3 **E**xplain how you determined your answers.

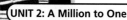

The Common Thread

1 **S**uppose you have one billion spools of thread and you want to store them in shoe boxes.

2 **H**ow many shoe boxes would it take?

3 **H**ow much space would be necessary to store all the shoe boxes?

4 **E**xplain how you determined your answers.

MENU
station
E

Taking Up Space

An office supply store needs to store a trillion sheets of paper.

1 How tall would a trillion sheets of paper be?

2 How much space would be needed to store that much paper?

3 Explain how you determined your answers.

Stepping Out

ou are a member of a hiking club. Your club would like to get its name printed in the "Incredible Book of Records" in order to attract new members to the club. To do so, they need one of their members to hike one million paces. That member is YOU!

Before starting your hike, you need to do some preparatory work. Think through and respond to each item below.

- Determine the length of your pace.

- Determine the length of one million of your paces.

- Decide on the route you would like to take to accomplish your goal of one million paces. Draw a detailed map of this route.

- Decide how much time it will take you to travel that distance and where you might stop if you need to sleep and eat along the way.

- Decide what food and supplies you will need to take on your trip and how you will carry them. Will you need help? If yes, when, where, and how much?

Write a report that includes the information above, along with the reasoning for each decision you made.

The Sports Locker

The Sports Locker, a major manufacturer of sports equipment, specializes in making playing balls for various sports: football, basketball, soccer, softball, volleyball, golf, and tennis.

The company wants to build a large warehouse to store one million of these playing balls. They have asked you, a group of architects, to come up with a detailed design of a warehouse large enough to store some of each type of playing ball. Due to cost and space limitations, the building must be a reasonable size that you can justify.

Working together with your group, determine how many playing balls of each type the company will store. Calculate how much space will be required to efficiently store the playing balls. Design a warehouse, including the dimensions. Write a justification for your design and be prepared to share it with the class.

ANT GOES CLIMBING

1.5 mm

An ant climbs to the top of the tallest building in Manhattan, the World Trade Center. The ant is seven millimeters long, and the World Trade Center is 1,350 feet tall. If the ant moves 1.5 millimeters each time it takes a step, how many steps must the ant take to climb from the base to the top of the World Trade Center?

If the ant can walk at a rate of six steps per second, how long will it take the ant to climb the skyscraper?

If ants were lined up from end to end, how many ants would it take to reach the top of the skyscraper? Draw a graph illustrating the size of the ant in relationship to the World Trade Center.

Suppose you took a trip and walked the same number of steps that the ant took. Where would you be in relation to your house? Illustrate your trip along with that of the ant's. Use a graph to show the comparison.

Be prepared to share your graphs with the class.

COMPUTER investigation

NPUT DATA ENT
OAD SAVE BACK
LOPPY DISK KE
OARD MOUSE HA
RIVE DOS MEMO
RGRAMS FILES

Spending Spree
Beat the Clock

You have just been awarded a billion dollars. Congratulations! In order to keep the money, you must abide by the following conditions.

Condition 1: You must save half of your money.

Condition 2: You have exactly three days to spend the other half of the money. You may spend your money on anything, but each item you buy must belong to one of the following eight categories.

- real estate
- transportation
- travel
- personal (clothes, food, jewelry, cosmetics, and so on)
- recreation
- equipment (furniture, electronic equipment, appliances, and so on)
- charity
- other

You may not spend more than 12% of the billion dollars in any one category. You must identify the source of each expense.

If you fail to spend all your money in three days, you will lose it all!

When the Shopping Gets Tough, The Tough Use a Computer

If your computer has software for spreadsheets, you can use it to keep track of the amount of money you spend in each category.

Start by entering the amount of money you estimate you will spend in each category. Enter the estimates in the row labeled "Budget Amount." The far column to the right keeps a total of the amount entered. Remember not to budget more than 12% of the total in any category except savings.

Research what you want to buy. You can find the price of items from various sources such as newspaper advertisements, catalogs, real estate information, travel brochures, and so on. For each item you purchase, enter the amount in the appropriate category. Once you select an item, enter the name of the item in a row under the "Description." Enter the price under the corresponding category in the same row. The computer will automatically total the number in the columns and display the balance in each column as well as the totals. Continue the process of entering items and their purchase price until all your money is spent. Remember you have three days to spend all of the money or you will lose it.

Write a report explaining your purchases. Explain the process you used. Illustrate how you spent your money with graphs or other pictorial representation.

COMPUTER investigation

Trip to Pluto

Your group is a planning crew for NASA. Your assignment is to plan a trip to the planet Pluto.

Some questions you need to consider are listed below.

- How many astronauts will be aboard?

- How fast will the spacecraft travel?

- How long will it take to travel to and from Pluto?

- What supplies will the astronauts need to take on their trip?

- How much storage space will they need on the spacecraft?

Refer to your Data Bank for information about planets and space travel. Develop a plan for the trip to Pluto, including in it your responses to the questions above. Design a timeline showing the stages of the trip. This timeline may include the points at which the spacecraft passes other planets and the length of time the astronauts stay on Pluto. Be prepared to share your plan, along with the reasoning for your decisions.

Library of Congress

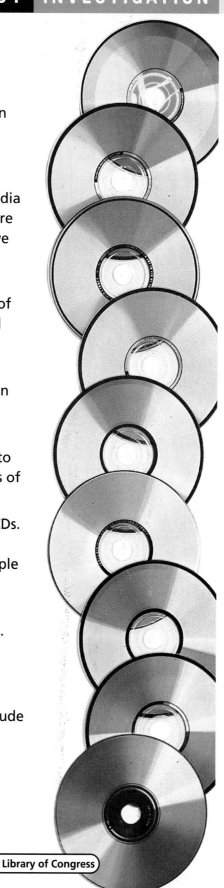

You work for the Library of Congress, the largest library in the United States. This library contains books, manuscripts, photographs, audio materials, and video materials.

Recently, you recommended to Congress that electronic media could save the library a lot of space. It would also allow more people to have access to the information and safely preserve the contents of all this information.

Congress asks you to develop a plan to convert the Library of Congress into an electronic media center. This center would transmit all information through computers with CD-ROM, modems, laser-disc players, and music CD players.

- Using your Data Bank, find the amount of information in the Library of Congress and the amount of information that can be digitally stored on a CD.

- Determine the number of CDs that would be necessary to store the contents of the books, films, and other sources of information in the Library of Congress.

- Determine the amount of space necessary to store the CDs. Draw a floor plan of your electronic media center, indicating where the CDs may be stored and where people could come to use the information.

- Compare the size of your media center to that of the Library of Congress. Use graphs to show the comparison. Explain why it would be advantageous to convert the Library of Congress into an electronic media center.

Prepare an oral presentation of your plan for Congress. Include your floor plan of the media center and your comparison graphs. Explain your calculations and justify your plan.

THE RECYCLING PROJECT

Our Earth's resources are not endless. We need to do our part in reducing waste and saving our planet. This recycling project will show you how much you can do to protect our planet.

Research how much waste is handled in the community in which you live. Find out if there are any recycling efforts currently in place.

Select a household item to recycle. It could be aluminum cans, newspapers, plastic bottles, glass, motor oil, clothes, or any other recyclable item. Collect as many of that item as you can around your home.

Write a statement describing the need to recycle that item. Estimate how much space is required to store one million items. Estimate how much time it would take you to collect that many items. Estimate how much time it would take your community to collect that many items. Then estimate how much money you could earn by recycling.

Interview an adult outside of school and ask him or her what he or she would consider in doing this recycling project.

Collect the items for a couple of weeks. Using that sample, respond to the following questions.

- How much space would it take to store one million items?

- How much space would be saved from the dumping of waste?

- How long would it take you to collect one million items?

- How long would it take your community to collect one million items?

- How much money would be earned in the recycling effort?

Consider how long it would take Americans to recycle one billion items and respond to the following questions.

- How much space would it take to store one billion items?
- How much space would be saved from the dumping of waste?
- How long would it take to collect one billion items?
- How much money would be earned in the recycling effort?

Consider these same questions for one trillion recyclable items.

Write a detailed report describing your process and conclusions. Make the report persuasive. Use graphs and/or charts to support your findings. This project is the major assessment for this unit, so you may want to do work outside of class.

Selection and Reflection

Part 1

In the beginning of this unit, your class started collecting milk lids. Using your collection as a sample, describe the size of a million, a billion, and a trillion in terms of the time it would take to collect the milk lids and the space it would take to store them. Use a graph to compare a million, a billion, and a trillion milk lids. During the first activity, you made estimates of this information. How do your estimates compare with your calculations today?

Part 2

Describe what you know about large and small numbers. When in the unit did you use mathematics? What did you learn while doing this unit? Use examples from several of the unit's activities in your responses.

The Problem

Your pen pal in Australia is sending you macadamia nuts for your birthday. She is sending enough nuts so that you can share them with your classmates. The macadamia nuts will arrive in boxes that measure 2 inches × 4 inches × 8 inches. If she sends 24 boxes, what size carton would she have to put them in? Are there other possibilities? Explain.

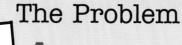

Take A Breather!

The Problem

About how many times will you breathe between today and this time next year?

Extension About how many times will your heart beat in the next 30 days?

The Problem

One Step Beyond

While attending the circus, Jimmy was quite impressed by the man walking on stilts. He began daydreaming about what it would be like to be that tall and what it would be like to be able to take such giant steps.

After he went to sleep that night, he began dreaming that he was walking on stilts. Jimmy's stilts were special. The first day he tried to walk on them, his first step was only one foot long. The second day he tried to walk on them, he was able to step two feet. The third day he stepped four feet, and he stepped 8 feet the fourth day. He realized that not only were his steps getting longer, they doubled the length of the step of the day before. If his steps continued to increase at this rate, how many miles will one step be in twenty-five days on his special stilts?

If Jimmy continues to walk in the same direction, what countries might he step into as he walks? Use a map. Then explain how this is possible.

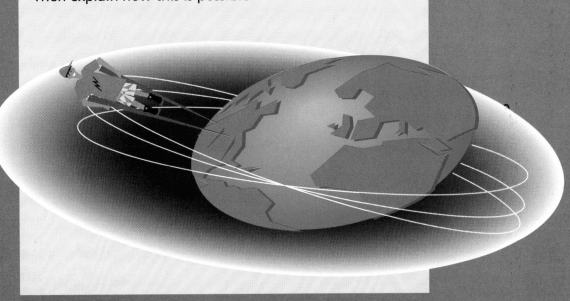

Space Cadets

The Problem

Suppose you travel on Spacey Airbus in the year 2275. They offer an incentive program to any space travelers who travel 401,720 miles within one year with them. You can earn free trips to other planets or the moon.

In six months, you have traveled only half the distance needed to earn a free trip. Regretably, you have no further plans to travel in the next six months.

Spacey Airbus cares about your business so they have offered another incentive plan for Earthlings. They will count every step you take on Earth as one mile of travel.

- How many steps will you need to take to make up the other half of the mileage?

- Can you take that number of steps in six months? How long will it take you? How many trips around a block would you have to make.

The Problem

Jamie bought a raffle ticket and she won! She put one-half of her winnings into her college savings plan. Two-thirds of the remainder must be paid in taxes. There is $500 left for her to spend. How much did she win?

Winning Ways

Pizza Puzzle

The Problem

There are seven astronauts aboard your spacecraft. One of your special meals consists of a large pizza. Can you cut the pizza into seven pieces (not equal in size) with just three straight cuts?

Extension A large wheel of cheese is also part of the food supply on the spacecraft. Can you cut the wheel into eight *equal* pieces with just three straight cuts?

TABLE OF CONTENTS

Metric System

1 centimeter (cm) = 10 millimeters (mm)

1 meter (m) = 100 cm or 1,000 mm

1 kilometer (km) = 1,000 meters

Customary System

1 foot (ft) = 12 inches (in.)

1 yard (yd) = 3 ft or 36 in.

1 mile (mi) = 5,280 ft

Equivalent Measures	
Metric System	Customary System
1 millimeter	0.039 inch
1 centimeter	0.39 inch
1 meter	39.37 inches
1 kilometer	0.62 miles

Equivalent Measures	
Customary System	Metric System
1 inch	2.54 centimeters
1 foot	30.48 centimeters
1 yard	0.9144 meter
1 mile	1.609 kilometers

Planets	Diameter	Average Distance from Sun	Number of Moons	1 Rotation*	Orbit*
Mercury	3,100 miles (4,987.0 km)	36 million miles (75.9 million km)	0	59 days	88 days
Venus	7,500 miles (12,067.5 km)	67 million miles (107.8 million km)	0	243 days	225 days
Earth	7,926 miles (12,752.9 km)	93 million miles (149.6 million km)	1	24 hours	365 days
Mars	4,218 miles (6,786.8 km)	142 million miles (228.5 million km)	2	24.4 hours	687 days
Jupiter	89,400 miles (143,844.6 km)	483 million miles (777.1 million km)	16	10 hours	11.86 years
Saturn	75,000 miles (120,675 km)	886 million miles (1,425.6 million km)	20	10.4 hours	29.46 years
Uranus	32,300 miles (51,970.7 km)	1.8 billion miles (2.9 billion km)	15	17 hours	84 years
Neptune	30,000 miles (48,270 km)	2.8 billion miles (4.5 billion km)	3	18-22 hours	165 years
Pluto	1900 miles (3,057.1 km)	3.7 billion miles (5.95 billion km)	1	6.4 days	248 years

*Hours, days, and years are Earth time.

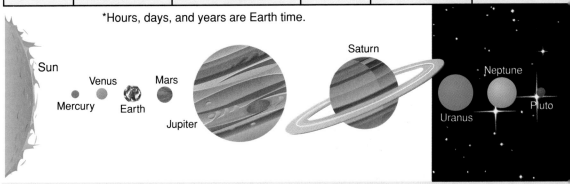

To reach a planet located closer to the sun than Earth, the rocket must travel in the opp▮ direction from the orbit of Earth at a speed of 0.4 miles per second less than the speed ▮ Earth. That makes the speed of the rocket about 65,160 miles per hour.

To reach a planet located farther from the sun than Earth, the rocket must travel in the ▮ direction as Earth and at a speed of 0.4 miles per second more than the speed of Earth. ▮ would make the speed of the rocket about 68,040 miles per hour.

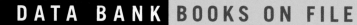

The Library of Congress

The Library of Congress In Washington, D.C., is the largest library in the United States.

In addition to being a reference library for the members of Congress and other government officials, the Library of Congress provides numerous services. It serves as the national center for service to the blind and issues books in braille and audio-recorded books. The library also has a record of the volumes contained in 2,500 other libraries.

The huge collection of books, manuscripts, music, prints, maps, and video and audio materials is housed in three buildings. These buildings contain 2,813,000 square feet (261,609 square meters) of floor space.

If you lined up all of the shelves in the library, you would have 2,807,775 feet (855,810 meters), or about 532 miles (856 kilometers), of shelves.

As of 1992, there are 28,000,000 books, 35,000,000 original manuscripts, 13,876,482 photographs, 691,459 films and videos, and 1,818,029 audiotapes.

Source: the Library of Congress

Storing Information on a CD-ROM

CD-ROM stands for Compact Disc—Read Only Memory.

One CD-ROM contains 650 megabytes of memory. It is $4\frac{3}{4}$ inches (120 mm) in diameter.

A CD-ROM disc can store many different types of media:
- 270,000 typed pages of manuscript
- 1,500 standard computer floppy disks
- 20 volumes of an encyclopedia
- 5,000 photographs
- 74 minutes of video
- 72 minutes of audio

Source: 3-M Company

GLOSSARY INDEX

P

Paces, 15
Points, 20
Predictions, 1
Problem solving, 4, 5, 8

R

Rate, 1, 17, 27
Reasoning, 15, 20
Relationship, 4, 17
Relative size, 1
Research, 19, 22
Rotation, 33
Rounded, 7

S

Savings, 19
Scientific notation, 7
Second, 17
Size, 16, 17, 21, 24, 25
Software, 19

Spreadsheets, 19
Square feet, 34
Square meters, 34

T

Time, 15, 20, 24, 26, 33
Timeline, 3, 20
Total, 19

W

Weeks, 22
Weight, 2, 3

Y

Yard, 32
Year, 2, 3, 26, 28, 33

Z

Zeros, 7, 8

COVER, Roy Morsch/The Stock Market;

iii, **1**(l), John Moreno/Lost Images, (r), **2**(l), Aaron Haupt Photography, (t), John Moreno/Lost Images; **3**(t), Scott Cunningham, (r), Aaron Haupt Photography, (screened), William Kennedy/The Image Bank, (cl), Erich Hartmann/Magnum Photos, (cr), Courtesy Youth For Environmental Sanity, Santa Cruz, CA, (bl), Larry Hamill, (br), K S Studios/Bob Mullenix; **4-5**(b), Chris Rogers/The Stock Market; **4**(tr), Hermann Eisenbeiss/Photo Researchers, (all others), Scott Cunningham; **5**(t), **6**, Hermann Eisenbeiss/Photo Researchers; **7**(t), Scott Cunningham, (bl), Crown Studios, (br), Hermann Eisenbeiss/Photo Researchers; **8**(t), Hal Yeager/FPG, (b), Hermann Eisenbeiss/Photo Researchers; **9, 11, 12, 13, 14**, Aaron Haupt Photography; **15**(l), Mark Newman/Photo Researchers (r), file photo; **16**(l), Tom Carroll/FPG, (r), Richard Fukuhara/Westlight; **17**, The Telegraph Colour Library/FPG; **18**, Life Images; **19**, Frank Fisher/WestStock; **20**(l), NASA, (r), Aaron Haupt Photography, (b), NASA/Science Source/Photo Researchers; **21**, K S Studios/Bob Mullenix; **22**(l), Gary E. Holscher/AllStock, (r), David Frazier; **23**, **24**(l), Aaron Haupt Photography, (inset), (r), Alan Carey; **25**, Crown Studios; **26**, BLT Productions/Brent Turner; **28**, Photri/The Stock Market; **29**, Frank Fisher/WestStock; **31**, Photri/The Stock Market; **32**, BLT Productions/Brent Turner; **33**, Paul Ambrose/FPG; **34**, Aaron Haupt Photography.